NOT JUST A TEACHER A FUCKING LEGEND

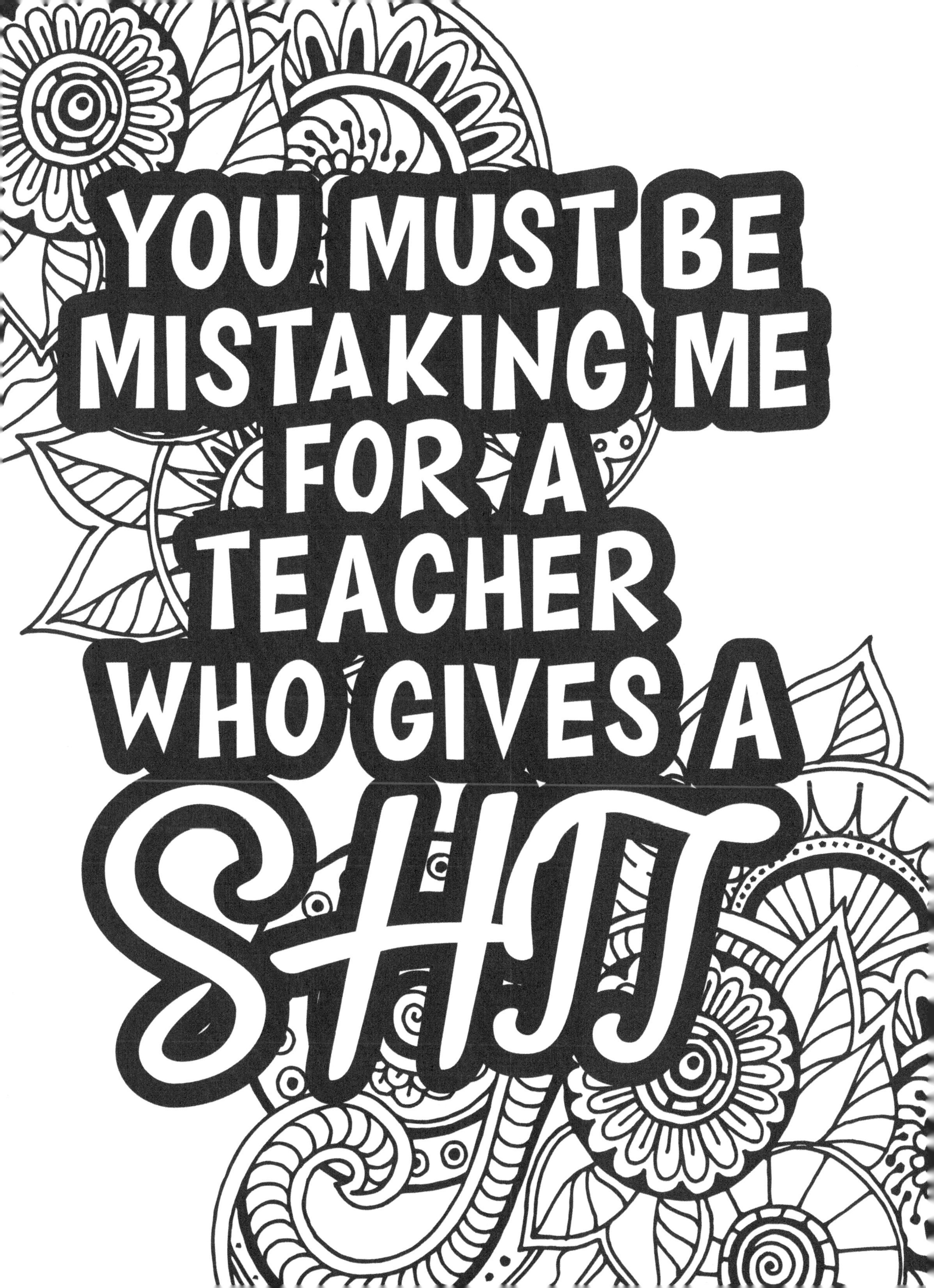
YOU MUST BE
MISTAKING ME
FOR A
TEACHER
WHO GIVES A
SHIT

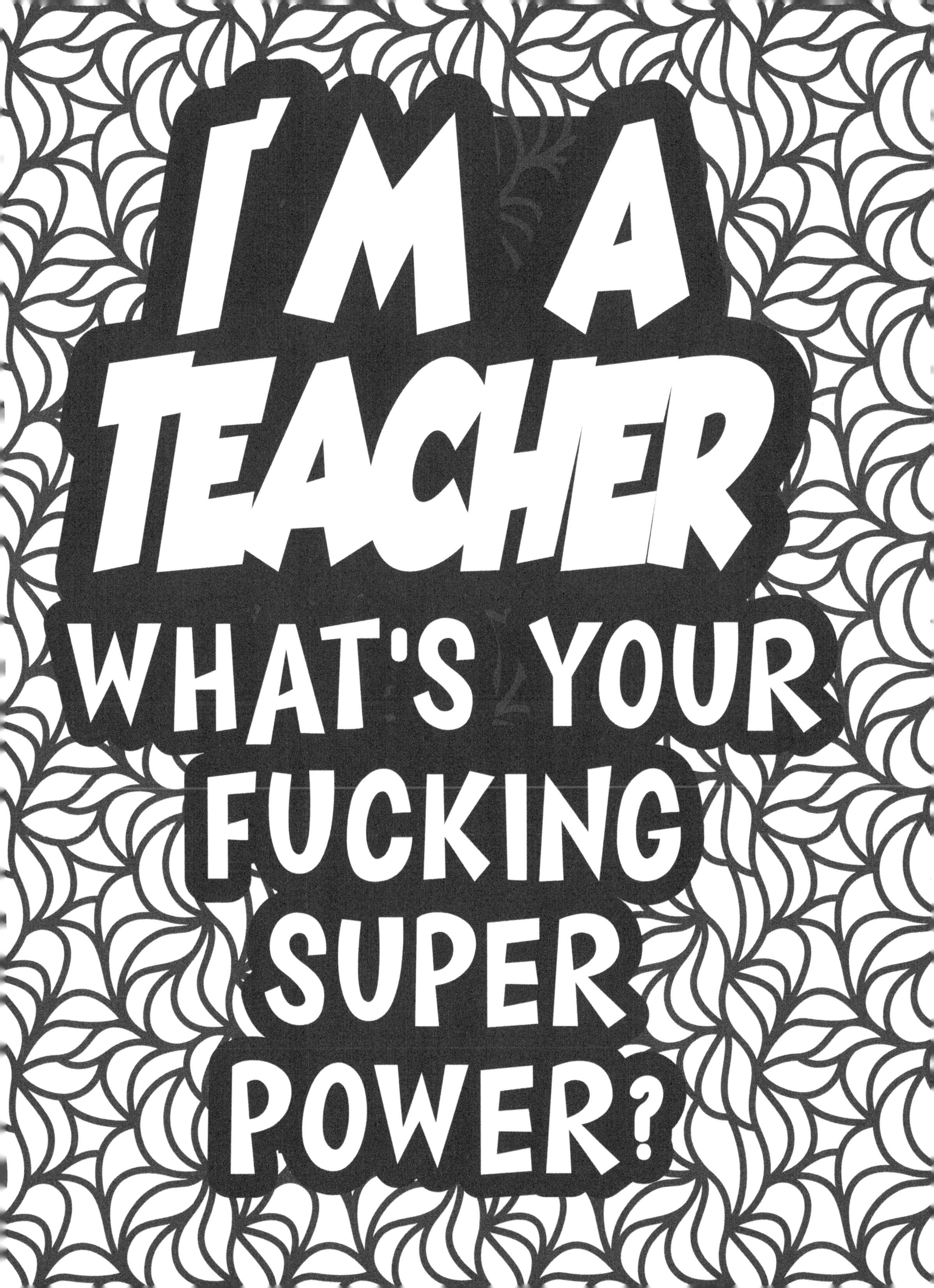
I'M A
TEACHER
WHAT'S YOUR
FUCKING
SUPER
POWER?

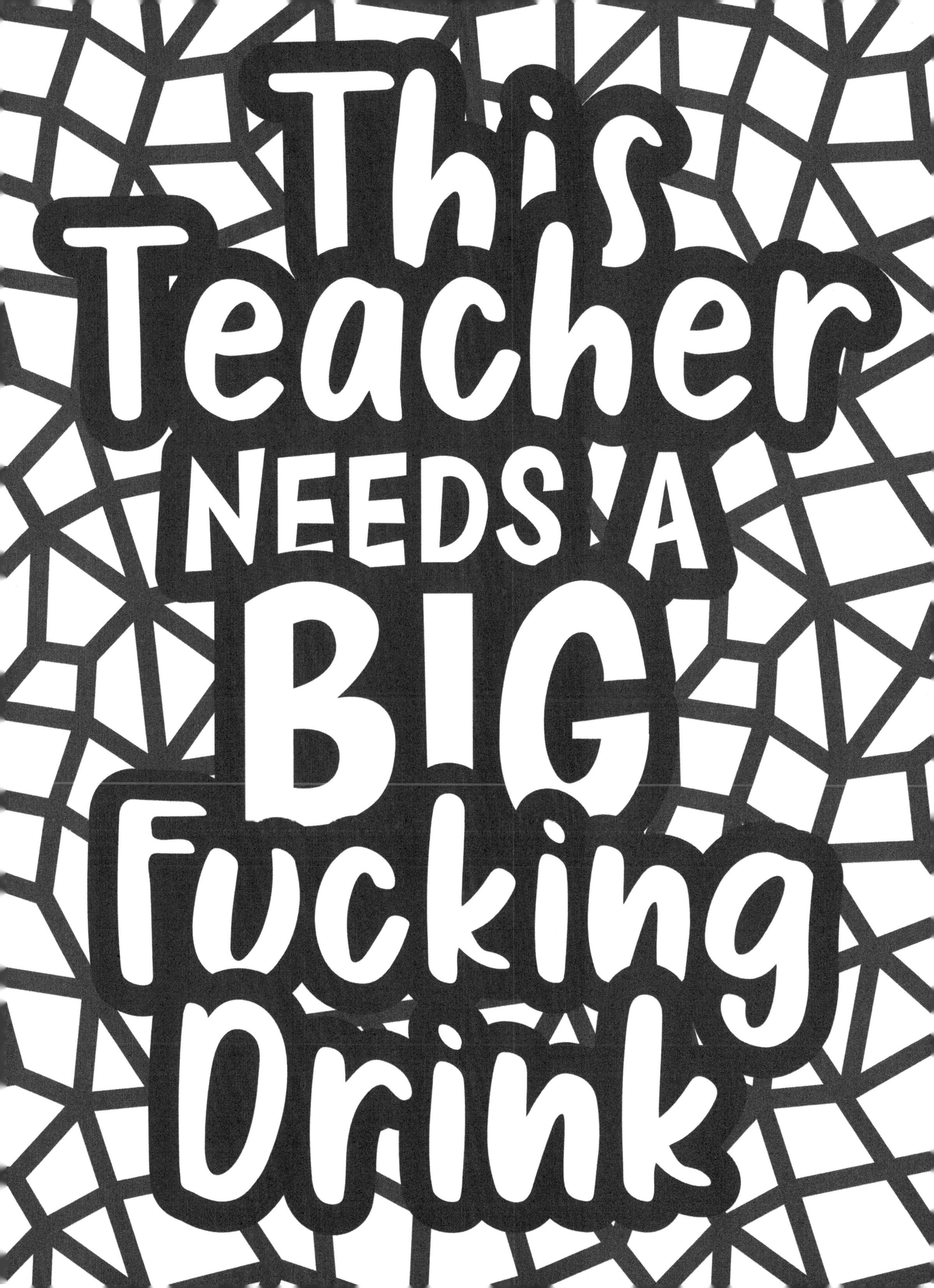
This Teacher NEEDS A BIG Fucking Drink

BOLLOCKS

Oh Dear

I forgot to give a fuck.

HAPPY AS
FUCK

SORRY

I'M DONE HELPING ASSHOLES TODAY

FUCK
OFF

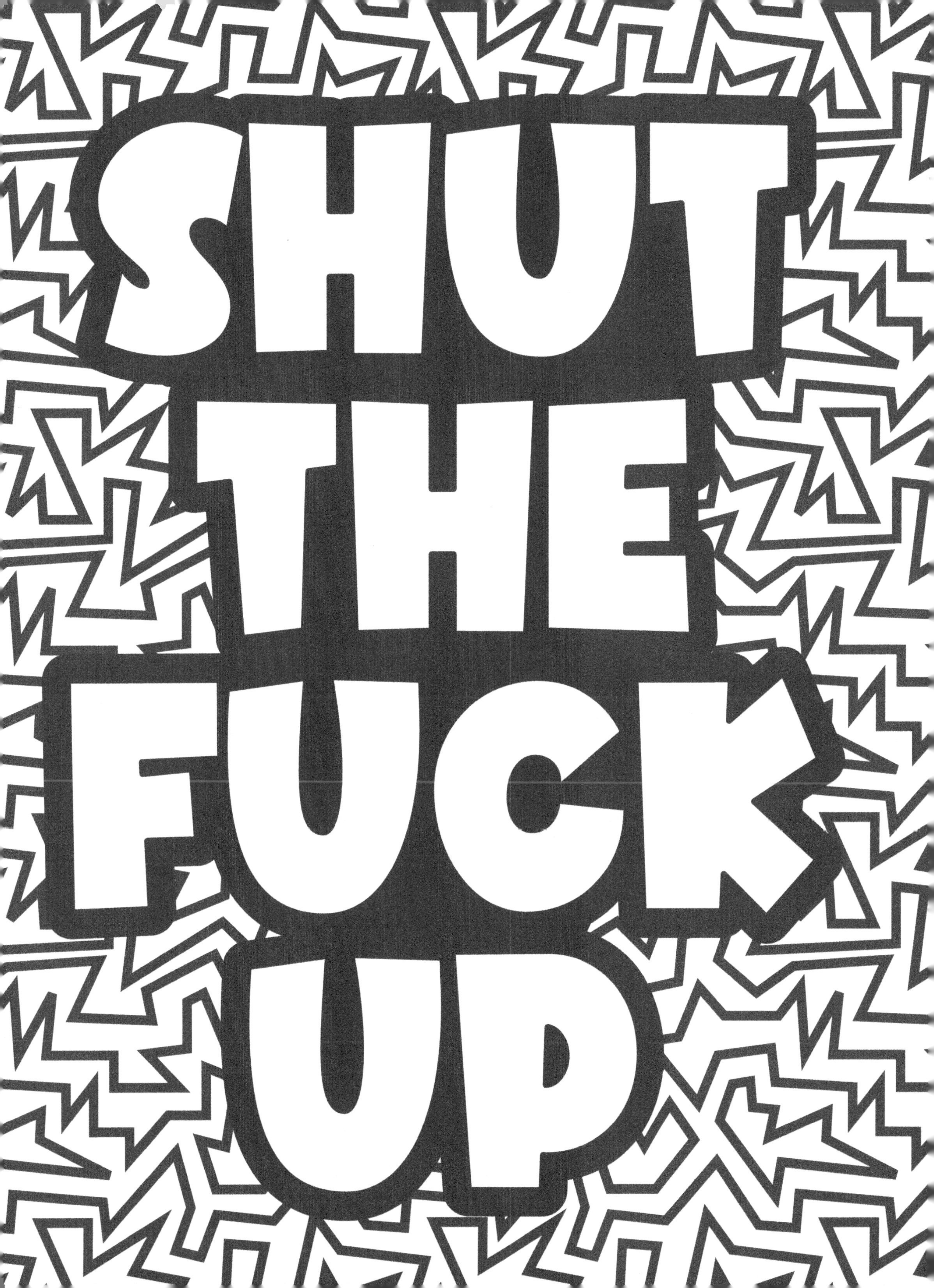
SHUT
THE
FUCK
UP

NO
SHIT

STUDIES HAVE
SHOWN THAT
INTELLIGENT PEOPLE
SWEAR MORE THAN
STUPID
MOTHERFUCKERS

I'VE GOT
A BAD
CASE OF THE
FUCK
ITS

KEEP
CALM
AND
FUCK
IT

Listen.
Smile.
Agree.

THEN DO WHATEVER
THE FUCK YOU WERE
GOING TO DO ANYWAY

I DON'T LIKE
MORNING
PEOPLE
OR
MORNINGS
OR
PEOPLE

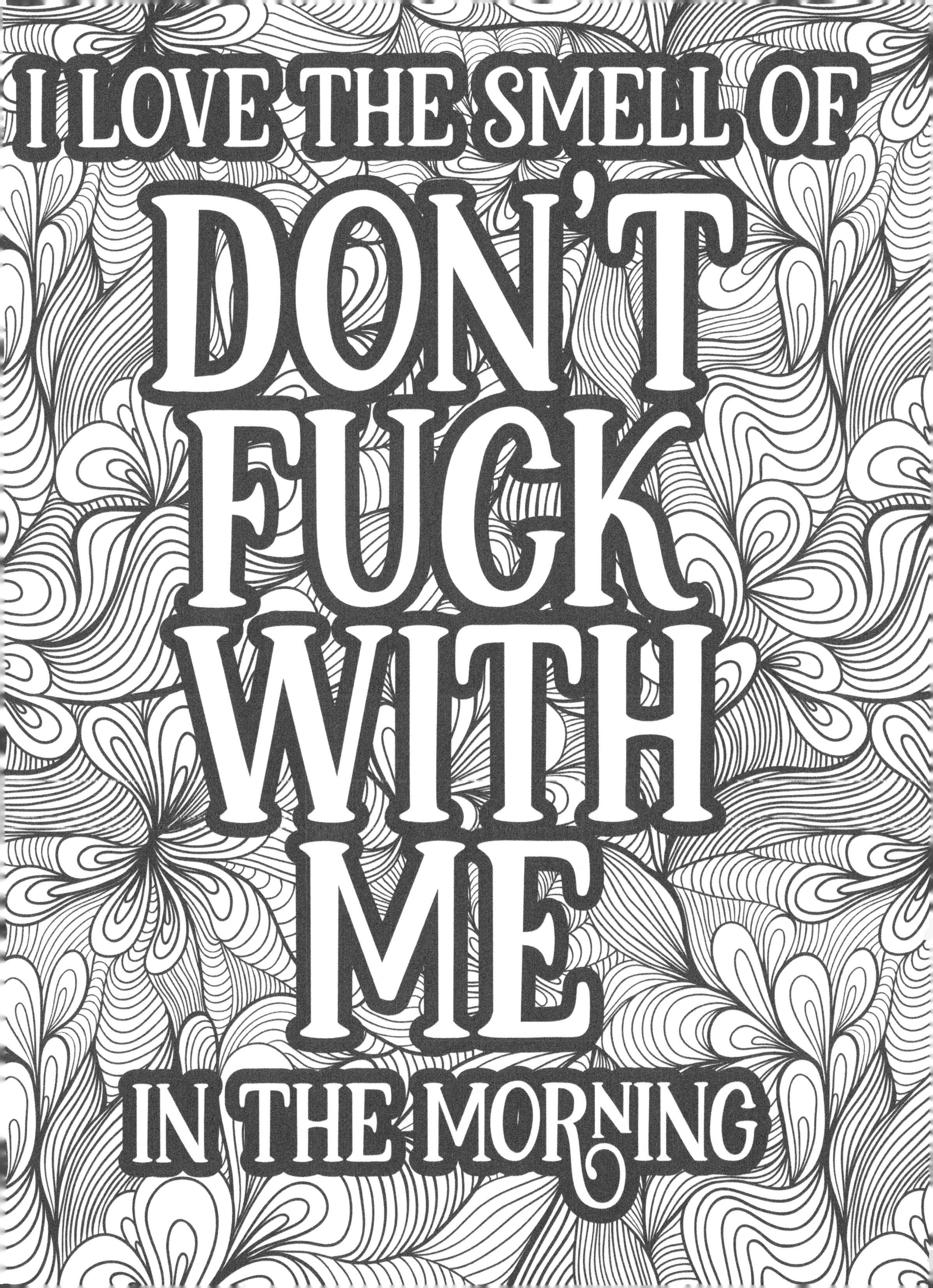
I LOVE THE SMELL OF
DON'T
FUCK
WITH
ME
IN THE MORNING

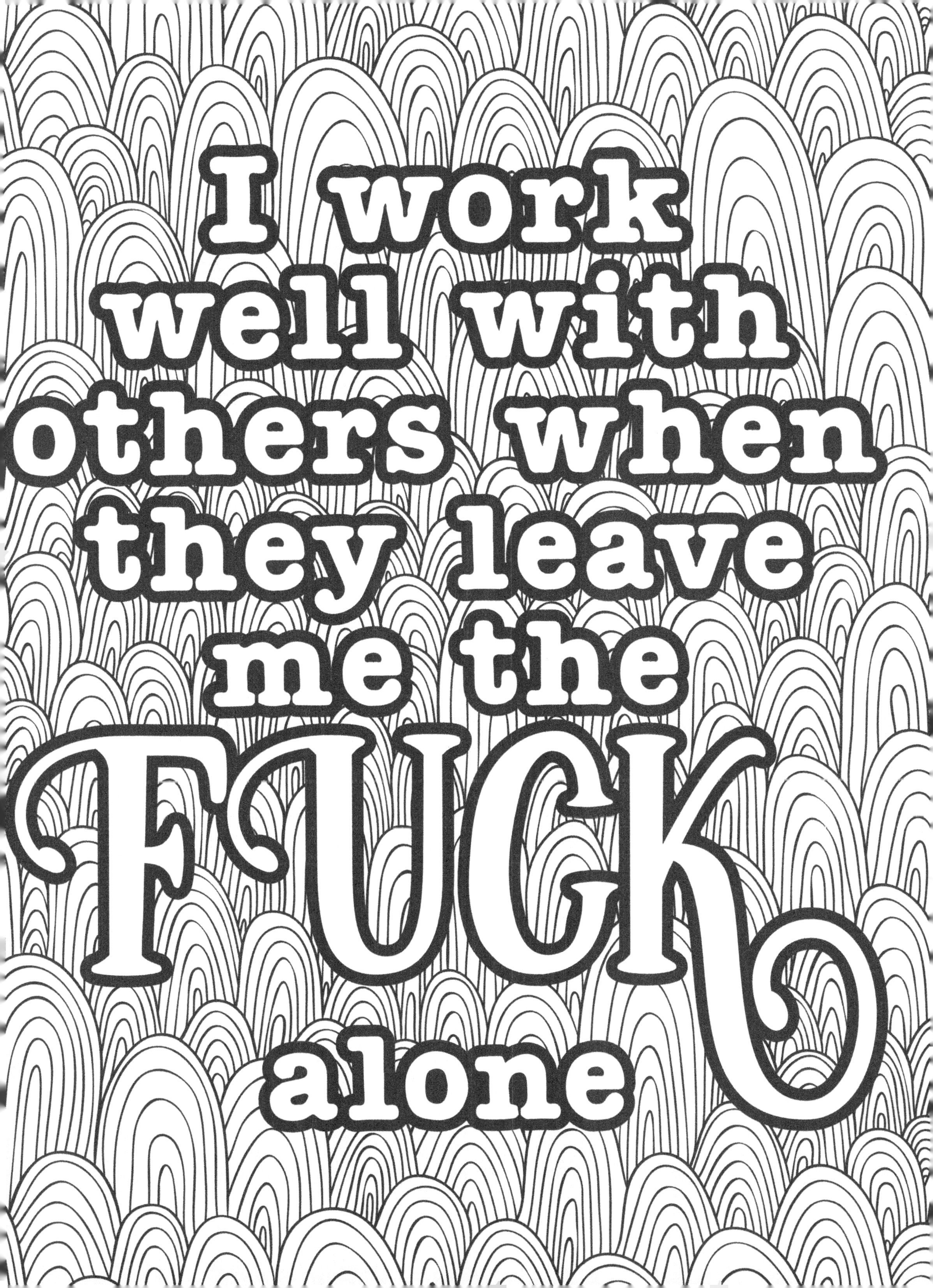
I work
well with
others when
they leave
me the
FUCK
alone

I
DON'T
FUCKING
CARE

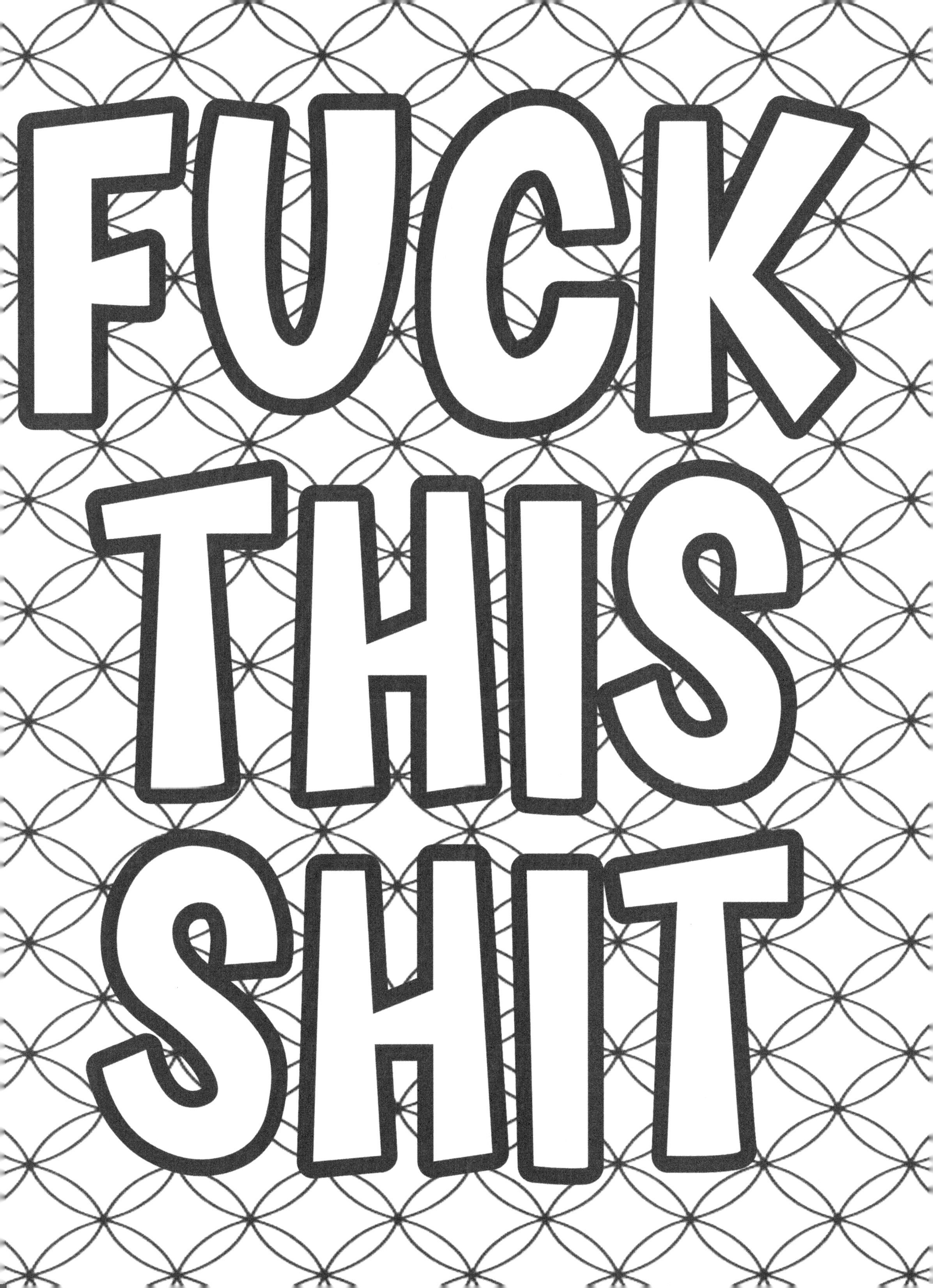
FUCK
THIS
SHIT

THE ONLY PERSON
I'M AFRAID OF IS
MYSELF
THAT FUCKER IS
CRAZY

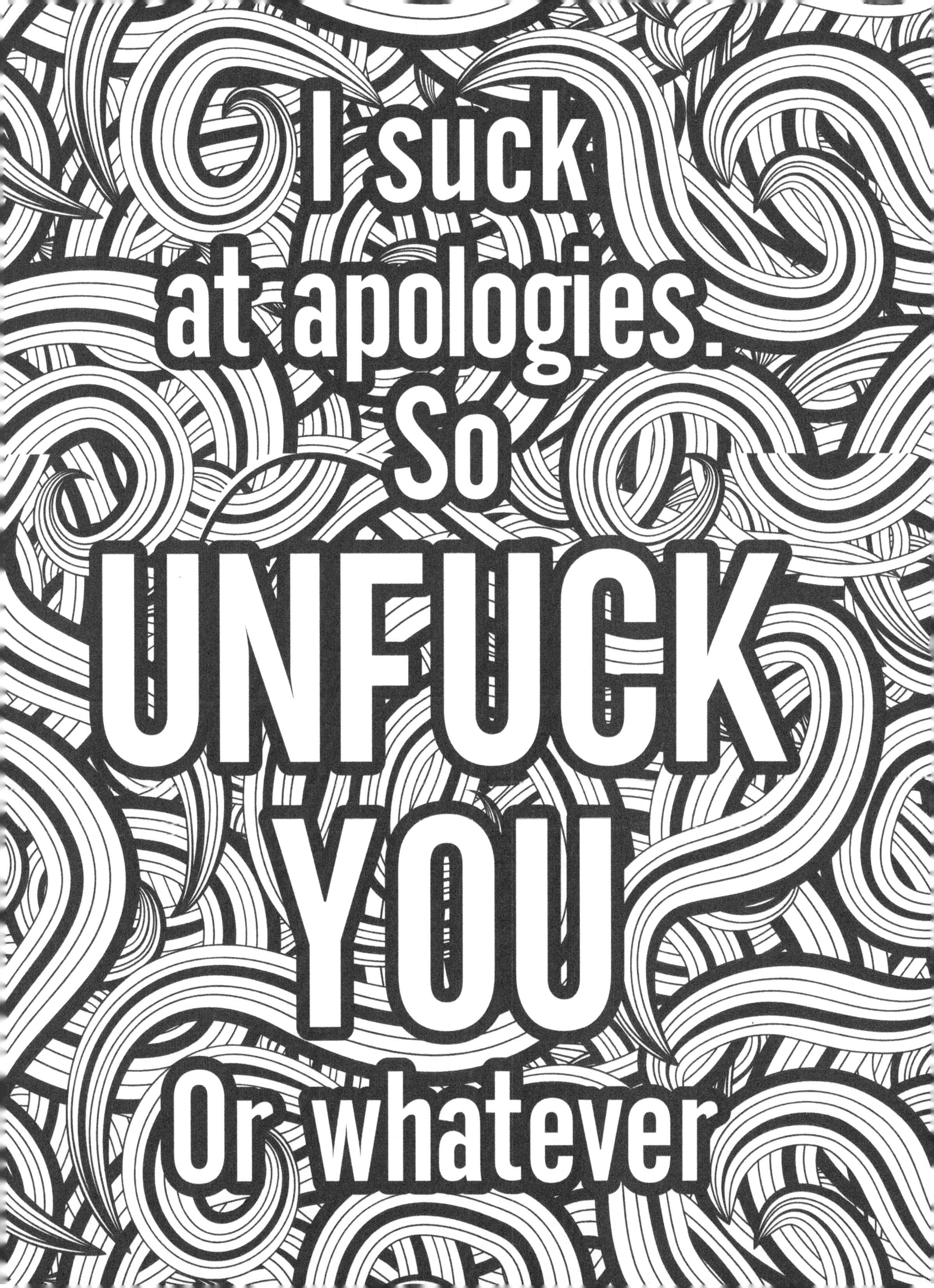
I suck
at apologies.
So
UNFUCK
YOU
Or whatever

CLASSY
AS
FUCK

WHEN I SAY
HAVE A NICE
DAY
REMEMBER
THAT THE
"FUCKER"
IS SILENT.

WHO THE

FUCK

TOOK MY...

OH. HERE IT IS.

I DON'T HAVE
TRUST ISSUES.
I JUST THINK
MOST PEOPLE
ARE FULL OF
SHIT.

I WONDER
IF LIFE
SMOKES
ME
AFTER IT
FUCKS ME

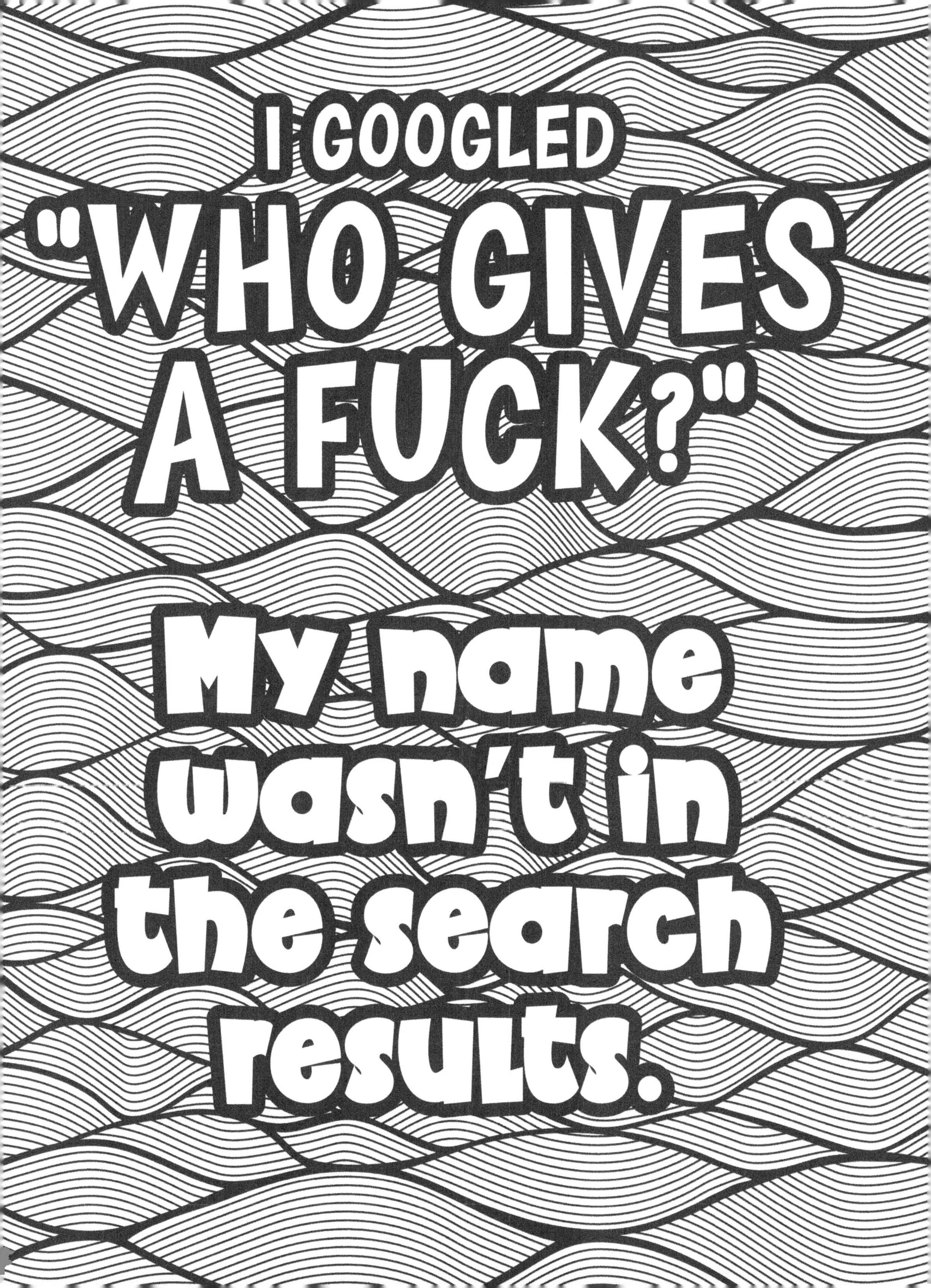
I GOOGLED
"WHO GIVES
A FUCK?"
My name
wasn't in
the search
results.

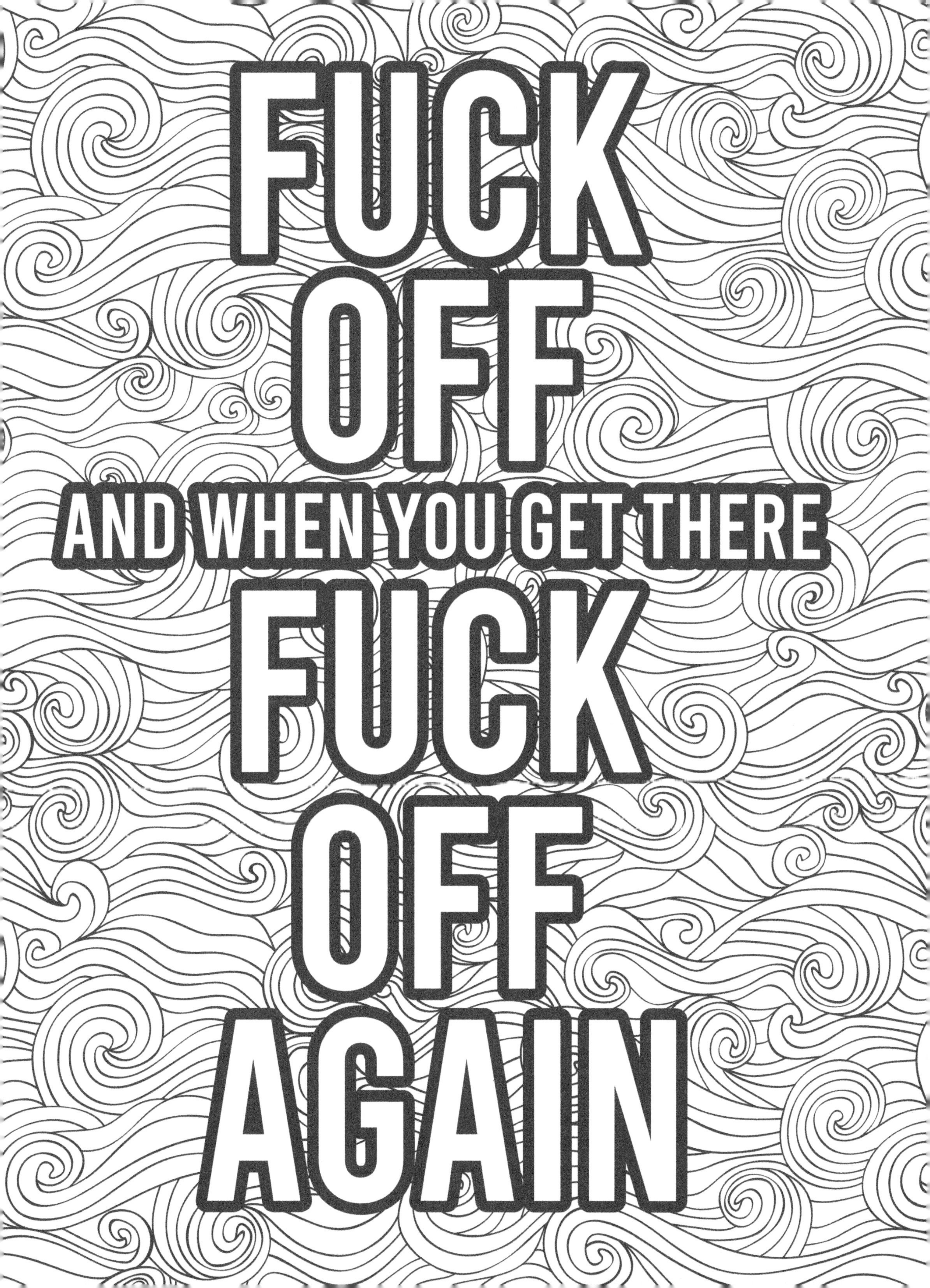
FUCK
OFF
AND WHEN YOU GET THERE
FUCK
OFF
AGAIN

Oh look...

Five minutes into work and I'm already irritated as

Fuck.

Sassy
Classy
and still kicking
Assy

THE PATH OF INNER PEACE BEGINS WITH FOUR WORDS

NOT MY FUCKING PROBLEM

HANG ON
I'M STILL DECIDING
IF I DON'T GIVE A
SHIT
OR IF I DON'T GIVE A
FUCK

I DON'T HAVE
ENOUGH
COFFEE
OR
MIDDLE
FINGERS
TODAY

Sorry
for being late.
I GOT CAUGHT UP
IN MY LAST FEW
MINUTES OF
NOT BEING HERE.

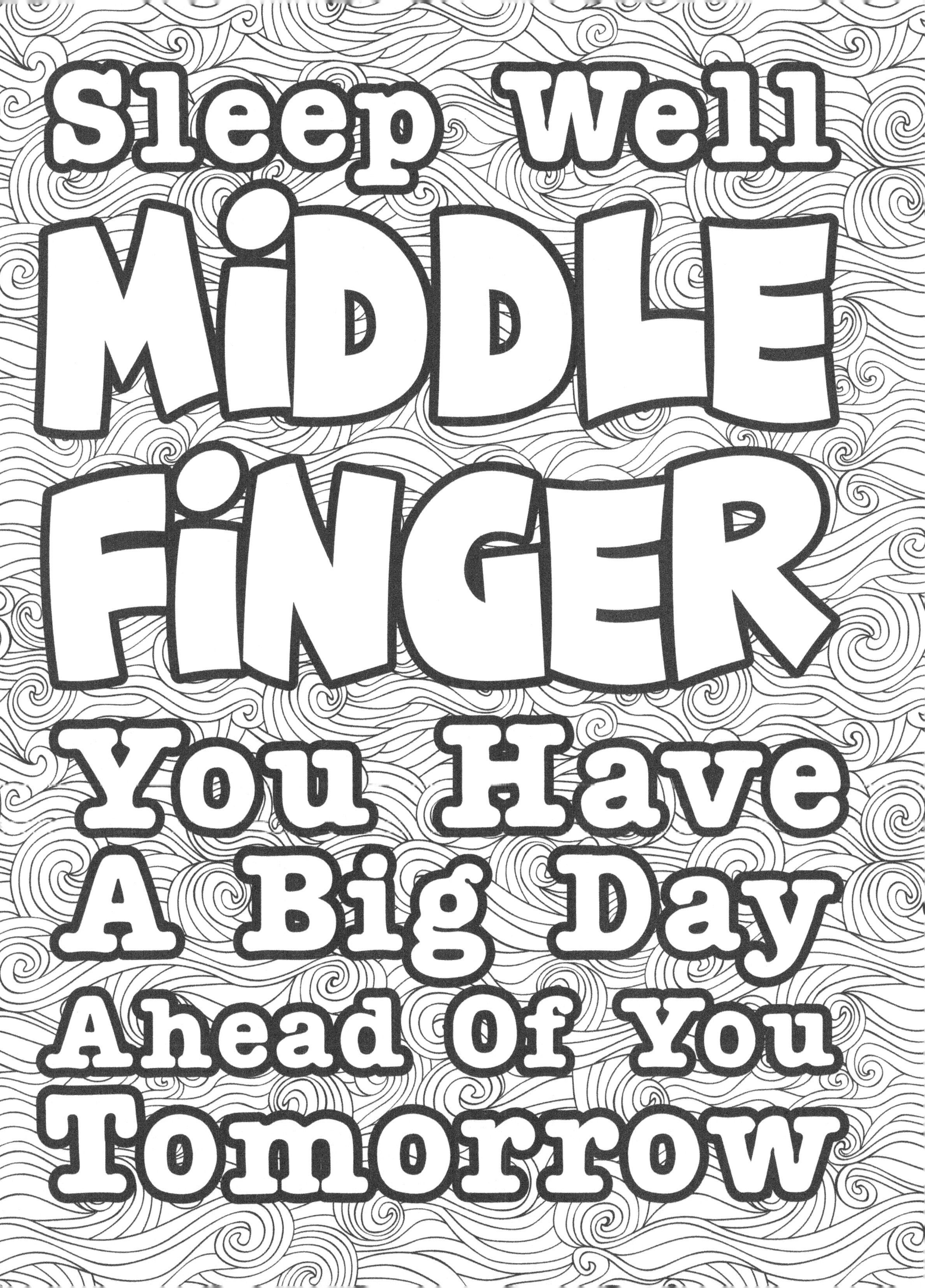
Sleep Well
MIDDLE
FINGER
You Have
A Big Day
Ahead Of You
Tomorrow

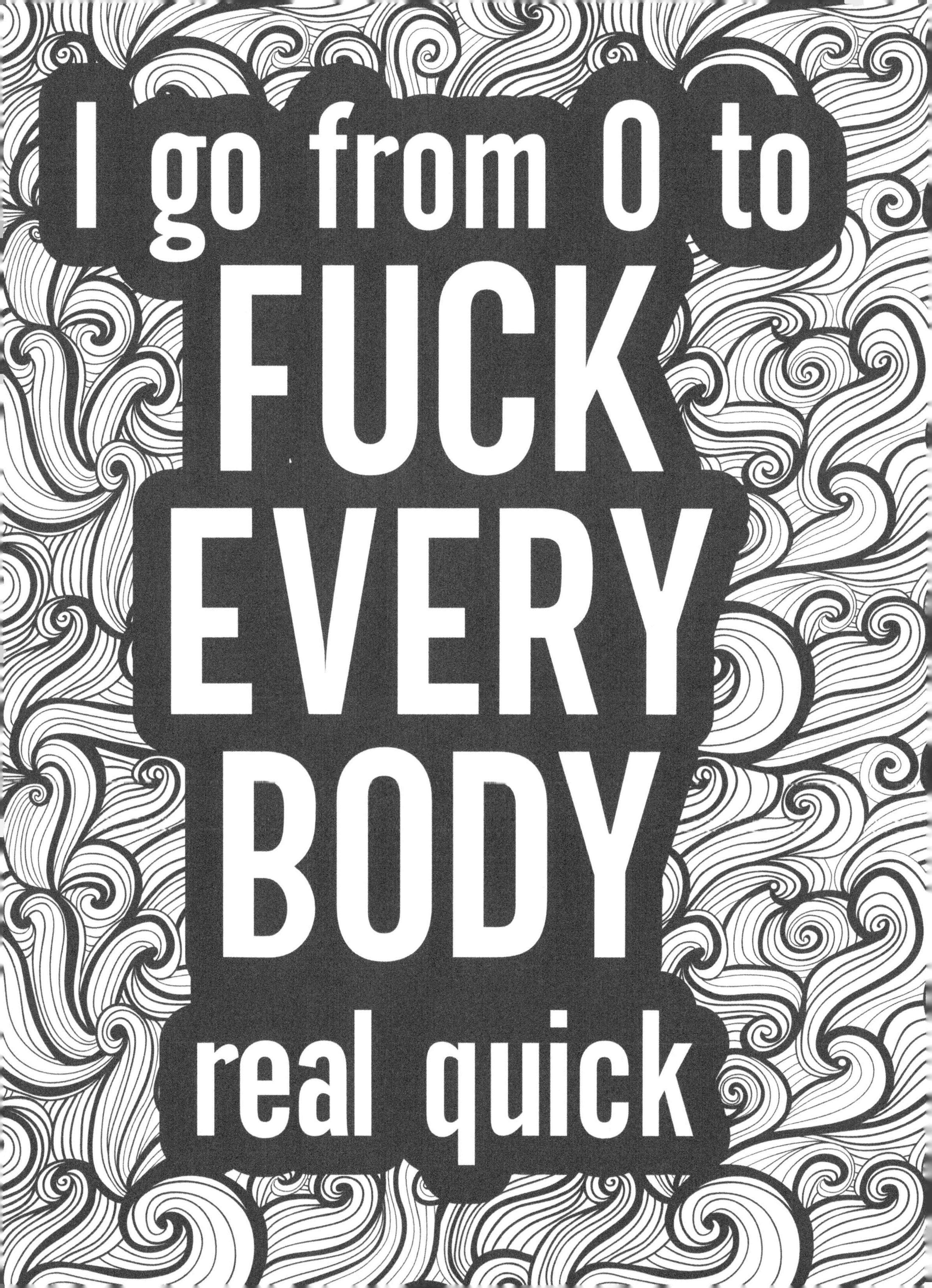
I go from 0 to
FUCK
EVERY
BODY
real quick

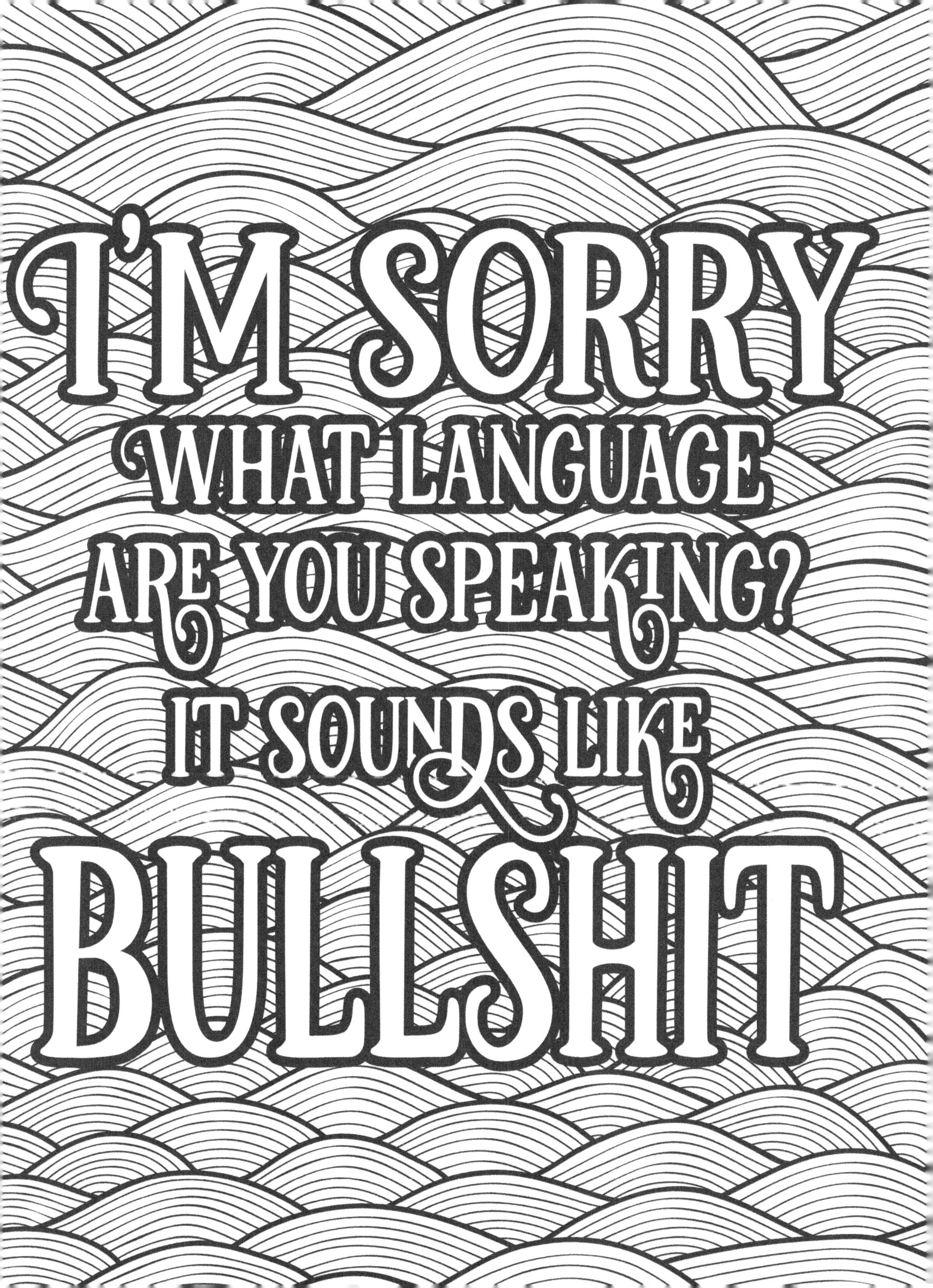
I'M SORRY
WHAT LANGUAGE
ARE YOU SPEAKING?
IT SOUNDS LIKE
BULLSHIT

I am
silently
correcting
your
shitty-ass
grammar.

BITCH,
Please

I
Swear
BECAUSE
I
care

CAN YOU HEAR THE SOUND
OF ME NOT GIVING A FUCK?

Abso
fucking
lutely

Get
Shit
Done

BULLSHIT
THE STRUGGLE
is
REAL

FUCK
THIS
SHIT

WHAT
THE
FUCK?

Damn
you all
to hell

INHALE
THE GOOD SHIT
EXHALE
THE BULLSHIT

FUCKITY
FUCK
FUCK
FUCK

Made in the USA
Las Vegas, NV
24 May 2021

23557850R00057